The Blue-Ringed Octopus

What you need to know More About the Greater Blue-ringed Octopus, Biology, Behaviour, and Habitats

Javier Smith

The Blue-Ringed Octopus

What you need to know More About the **Greater Blue-ringed Octopus,** Biology, Behaviour, and Habitats

Javier Smith

Diclaimer!!!

This book's content is solely intended for general informative purposes. Despite having taken every precaution to guarantee the authenticity and completeness of the material provided, the author disclaims all liability for any mistakes, omissions, or inconsistencies. At the time of publication, the information was based on the most recent research and understanding of the topic. Any loss or damage, whether direct, indirect, or consequential, caused or claimed to be caused by the use or application of any material in this book is expressly disclaimed by the author and publisher. It is recommended that readers check the material and, if necessary, consult a specialist.

The author's ideas and opinions are the only ones that matter in this book; they don't always represent the official policies or stance of any other firm, agency, or employment. This book is not meant to be a substitute for expert counsel in any field, including law or medicine. You agree to this disclaimer and confirm that you have read it by using this book.

Table of content

Introduction

The blue-ringed octopus possesses a complex charm that blends elements of danger, mystery, and beauty. With its remarkable appearance, this little cephalopod—which is frequently no bigger than a golf ball—commands attention. Bright, iridescent blue rings that seem to glow are all over its body; these rings are most noticeable when the octopus feels threatened. These striking symbols entice and warn at the same time, luring the viewer in with their mesmerizing beauty.

Beyond its outward appearance, the mysterious and secretive nature of the blue-ringed octopus captivates. It lives in the shallow waters of the Indian and Pacific Oceans, frequently hiding under coral reefs, cracks, and crevices. Because of its predilection for these isolated areas, it adds mystery to sightings, which makes them uncommon and thrilling experiences for divers and marine aficionados.

The blue-ringed octopus's reputation as one of the most poisonous animals in the water only serves to increase its attraction. It is small and has a delicate appearance, but its venom is strong enough to kill humans. It is a topic of both interest and terror due to its paradoxical beauty and lethality. The powerful neurotoxin tetrodotoxin, which can induce paralysis and, in extreme situations, death, is present in the octopus's venom. Because of its effective defense system, the blue-ringed octopus is a dangerous predator and a subject of great interest in toxicological and medical studies.

The octopus's intelligence and intricate behavior are further factors in its attraction. Blue-ringed octopuses are recognized for their ability to solve problems and sophisticated hunting strategies; these behaviors indicate a high degree of intelligence. Their ability to use tools, exhibit deft camouflage techniques, and solve puzzles adds to their mystery. It is possible to get insight into the cognitive capacities of cephalopods and the evolution of intelligence in the animal kingdom by observing these behaviors in their natural environment.

Furthermore, the blue-ringed octopus is a common symbol of both beauty and peril in many mythologies and civilizations. Its picture is often portrayed in literature, art, and other media, demonstrating its ongoing influence on people's imaginations. Its cultural relevance heightens its appeal and makes it a fascinating topic for researchers in a variety of areas.

To sum up, the blue-ringed octopus is a fascinating animal due to its amazing looks, enigmatic personality, deadly venom, sharp mind, and cultural influence. It is an amazing creature that captivates everyone who sees it, embodying the complexity and mysteries of the marine environment. The blue-ringed octopus never ceases to amaze and inspire us, whether it is through scientific research, artistic depictions, or firsthand observation. It serves as a constant reminder of the complexity and beauty of life beneath the seas.

Why Examine the Octopus with Blue Rings?

Researching the blue-ringed octopus takes researchers not only into the realm of marine biology but also into the realms of ecological significance, evolutionary ingenuity, and possible medical advances. The following are some strong arguments in favor of giving this amazing creature our scholarly attention:

1. Comprehending Toxicity and Venom: One of the strongest venoms known to science in the animal realm is produced by the blue-ringed octopus, and it contains the potent neurotoxin tetrodotoxin. Researching this venom may help create novel therapeutic interventions and counteragents by offering vital insights into the molecular mechanisms underlying it. Comprehending its venom can help improve our understanding of neurotoxins and how they affect the nervous system, which is important for study in pharmacology and medicine.

2. Perspectives on Evolution: Within the cephalopod family, the blue-ringed octopus exhibits a distinct evolutionary pathway. Scientists can learn more about the evolutionary processes that have shaped not only octopuses but also other marine animals by examining their genetic composition, behaviors, and adaptations. This information can aid in our comprehension of the more general mechanisms behind evolution and adaptability to changing environmental conditions.

3. Complexity of Behaviour: The blue-ringed octopus is one of the many octopuses that are recognized for their sophisticated behaviors and intellect. Examining a cephalopod's ability to solve problems, hunt, and connect with others can reveal important details about its cognitive makeup. These investigations, which provide analogies with other intelligent animals, including humans, advance our knowledge of animal intelligence and cognition.

4. Ecological Significance: As a predator and prey, the blue-ringed octopus is essential to its ecology. We can better understand the dynamics of these ecosystems and the equilibrium of marine life by examining its interactions within marine environments. The significance of maintaining a variety of healthy marine ecosystems is highlighted by this understanding, which is crucial for conservation efforts.

5. Awareness of the Environment and Conservation: Strategies for conservation aiming at preserving marine biodiversity can be informed by research on the blue-ringed octopus. Its habitat needs, dangers, and population dynamics must all be understood to create conservation plans that work. Furthermore, educating people about the blue-ringed octopus might pique their interest in marine conservation and the importance of safeguarding our seas.

6. Importance for Culture and Education:
Many cultures and educational programs have a special place in their hearts for the blue-ringed octopus. Public awareness of marine life and the value of its preservation can be increased by research on this species. Blue-ringed octopus-themed educational programs have the potential to increase public awareness of marine biology and inspire the next generation of scientists and conservationists.

7. Research in Biomedicine: There may be uses for the special qualities of the venom of the blue-ringed octopus in biomedical studies. Researchers are looking into the possibility of using venom components to create novel anesthetics, painkillers, and neurological disease treatments. The significance of this research is highlighted by the fact that studying such poisonous animals frequently results in advances in medical science.

To sum up, research on the blue-ringed octopus provides an insight into the wonders of the ocean, the complexities of poisonous adaptations, and the larger ecological and evolutionary backgrounds of this extraordinary species. Through studying the lives of the blue-ringed octopus, we not only learn more about this fascinating animal but also advance medical science, scientific understanding, and marine ecosystem protection.

Chapter One

Introducing the Blue-Ringed Octopus

The blue-ringed octopus, belonging to the genus **Hapalochlaena**, is a small but highly poisonous mollusk found in the coastal waters of the Pacific and Indian Oceans, mainly around Australia, Japan, Indonesia, and the Philippines. This genus has four recognized species: **Hapalochlaena maculosa**(Southern Blue-Ringed Octopus), **Hapalochlaena lunulata** (Greater Blue-Ringed Octopus), **Hapalochlaena fasciata** (Blue-Lined Octopus), and **Hapalochlaena nierstraszi**. Despite their diminutive size, usually measuring no more than 20 centimeters (8 inches) in length, including limbs, these octopuses are renowned for their vibrant blue and black rings and strong venom.

Physical Characteristics:

The blue-ringed octopus is instantly identified by its distinctive blue and black rings, which grow more visible when the animal is threatened or agitated. The rest of its body can vary in color, often ranging from yellowish to brown, allowing it to blend effortlessly into its surroundings when it is at rest. These color changes are facilitated by specialized skin cells called chromatophores, which can expand or shrink to alter the octopus's appearance.

- **Size:** Typically, blue-ringed octopuses are small, with a body length of around 4-5 centimeters (1.5-2 inches) and arm lengths that stretch up to 10 centimeters (4 inches).

- **Weight:** They are lightweight organisms, often weighing between 10 to 100 grams, depending on the species and maturity.

- **Rings:** The quantity and design of rings can vary among species, but they are usually brightly blue and appear iridescent due to the presence of multi-layer reflectors in the skin.

Unique Features and Markings:

One of the most stunning qualities of the blue-ringed octopus is its capacity to make an astounding display of iridescent blue rings. When at rest or disguised, the rings are hardly visible, but when the octopus feels threatened, these rings become brilliantly apparent, serving as a signal to potential predators. This exhibit is a typical example of aposematism, where brilliant colors are employed to communicate poison or danger.

Venom and Toxicity:

The blue-ringed octopus's venom is particularly strong and contains tetrodotoxin, a neurotoxin also present in pufferfish. Tetrodotoxin blocks sodium channels in nerves, preventing them from firing and leading to paralysis, respiratory failure, and potentially death if untreated. What makes their venom particularly hazardous is that it can be given through a painless bite, frequently unrecognized until symptoms begin to show.

- **Venom Delivery:** The octopus releases its venom through a beak placed in the center of its arms. This beak can pierce the shells of its prey, such as crabs and mollusks, injecting poison that paralyzes the victim.

- **Effects on Humans:** While bites are rare, they can be lethal. Symptoms in humans include numbness, muscle weakness, difficulty breathing, and paralysis. Immediate medical intervention is critical for survival.

Habitat and Distribution:

Blue-ringed octopuses are found in shallow, coastal waters, often at depths of up to 20 meters (66 feet). They frequent coral reefs, tide pools, and sandy or muddy bottoms where they can find adequate food supply and hiding spots. During the day, they often hide in nooks, shells, or under rocks to evade predators and relax.

Geographic Range: Their distribution extends across the western Pacific and Indian Oceans, with considerable populations near Australia, New Guinea, Indonesia, the Philippines, and Japan.

Environmental Preferences: They enjoy warm, tropical, and subtropical waters where they may merge into the colorful and diverse habitat of coral reefs.

Diet and Hunting Strategies:

The blue-ringed octopus is a voracious predator, eating mostly on small crustaceans, such as crabs and shrimp, as well as small fish and other marine invertebrates. It employs its venom not only for protection but also to immobilize victims.

Hunting Technique: The octopus hunts by pouncing on its prey and delivering a rapid bite with its beak, injecting venom that paralyzes the victim. It then uses its arms to manipulate and eat the prey.

Feeding Habits: After immobilizing its prey, the octopus utilizes its radula, a tongue-like device with microscopic teeth, to dig into the exoskeleton of crustaceans and ingest the soft tissues inside.

Reproduction and Life Cycle:
Blue-ringed octopuses have a relatively short lifespan of roughly one to two years. Their

reproductive behavior is intriguing and involves intricate mating rituals.

Mating: Mating occurs when a male approaches a female and inserts a specialized arm called the hectocotylus into the female's mantle cavity to transfer sperm packets.

Egg Laying: Females lay their eggs in a secure den and guard them until they hatch. The female does not feed during this phase and often dies shortly after the eggs hatch.

Development: The eggs hatch into planktonic larvae, which eventually settle on the ocean floor and grow into adults, completing the life cycle.

Conservation Status: Currently, blue-ringed octopuses are not classified as endangered, but their populations are sensitive to habitat loss, pollution, and human activities such as coastal development and tourism. Conservation activities are vital to ensure the protection of

their habitats and the broader marine ecosystems
they inhabit.

Chapter Two

The Wonder of Venom

Despite its diminutive size and generally peaceful look, the blue-ringed octopus is home to one of the strongest venoms in the animal kingdom. In addition to helping us understand the amazing cephalopod's evolutionary adaptations, understanding its venom and the mechanisms underlying its toxicity is also important for its ramifications in toxicology and medical science.

1. Venom's Composition: The main neurotoxin found in the venom of the blue-ringed octopus is called tetrodotoxin (TTX). Other marine animals including pufferfish, some new species, and some frogs are also known to contain aflatoxin. The octopus secretes this strong toxin, which builds up in several parts of the body, including the salivary glands, thanks to symbiotic bacteria.

Acidophilus (TTX): TTX prevents normal nerve impulse conduction by blocking voltage-gated sodium channels on the surface of nerve cells. The paralysis of muscles, including the respiratory muscles, results from this occlusion.

Accessory Elements: The venom may also include additional bioactive substances, such as enzymes that degrade tissues and aid in the toxin's dissemination, in addition to TTX.

2. Venom Delivery Mechanism:

The venom of the blue-ringed octopus is administered via its beak, which is situated in the middle of its arms. This beak can pierce the shells of crabs and other prey because it is robust and pointed.

Bite Process: The octopus injects venom into its beak through ducts after biting, drawing blood from two salivary glands. Usually painless, the bite may go unnoticed at first.

Impact on the Prey: The venom paralyzes the victim swiftly, which facilitates the octopus's ability to devour it. TTX causes fast immobilization in crustaceans by interfering with their neurological and muscular functions.

3. Venom's Effects on Humans:

Although human interactions are uncommon, blue-ringed octopus bites can be very harmful because of how strong their venom is. Enough TTX can be consumed in one bite to result in serious, possibly deadly symptoms.

Preliminary Signs: The symptoms, which could include breathing difficulties, muscle weakness, and numbness surrounding the bite site, might appear minutes to hours after the bite.

Degenerative Paralysis: Generalised muscle paralysis, including paralysis of the diaphragm and other breathing-related muscles, can be brought on by the toxin as it spreads. If left untreated, this might result in respiratory failure.

Additional Symptoms: Blurred vision, loss of coordination, nausea, and vomiting are possible side effects. Since TTX usually has no direct effect on the central nervous system, sufferers frequently maintain consciousness and awareness despite the severity of these symptoms.

4. First Aid and Treatment:

Anyone bitten by a blue-ringed octopus needs to get medical help right away. Since there isn't a recognized remedy for tetrodotoxin, supportive care is the mainstay of treatment.

Emergency Reaction: Make an instant call to emergency services. To stop the toxin from spreading, keep the person as motionless and composed as you can.

Assistive Respiratory: If the person is having trouble breathing, artificial respiration (CPR) can be required. In a hospital setting, mechanical breathing can be necessary until the person can breathe on their own and the toxin is broken down.

Care and Monitoring: In an intensive care unit, it's frequently necessary to provide supportive care in addition to ongoing vital sign monitoring. Depending on how severe the envenomation is, recovery may take several hours to several days.

5. The Function of Venom in Biology and Ecology: The blue-ringed octopus's venom performs both defensive and predatory roles.

- **Predation:** The main purpose of venom is to immobilize prey, which enables octopuses to capture and eat marine species with hard shells or those that are otherwise difficult to find.
- **Defence:** Potential predators are alerted to the brilliant blue rings. When larger assailants pose a threat, the octopus can neutralize or render them helpless with a poisonous bite.

6. Investigations and Possible Uses:

There may be uses for the research of tetrodotoxin and other elements of blue-ringed octopus venom in the scientific and medicinal domains.

Pain Management: Because TTX can block nerve signals, researchers are looking at it as a potential treatment for severe pain, especially pain associated with cancer.

Neuroscience Research: Knowledge of the relationship between TTX and sodium channels can help explain neurological diseases and nerve function.

Drug Development: The venom's ingredients could serve as the basis for brand-new drug classes intended to address ailments like chronic pain, cardiac arrhythmias, and epilepsy.

7. Viewpoint on Evolution:

The blue-ringed octopus's creation of such a strong venom is an amazing illustration of evolutionary adaptation.

- **Symbiosis:** The octopus and the bacteria that make TTX have a symbiotic relationship that exemplifies mutualism, in which both organisms gain from the toxin's manufacture and application.
- **-Specific Benefit:** The blue-ringed octopus's capacity to create and distribute strong venom probably offers substantial survival advantages, enabling it to fend off predators and effectively catch prey.

Knowing the blue-ringed octopus's toxicity and venom illustrates a complicated interaction between biology, ecology, and evolution. Despite being harmful, its venom provides important insights into neurology and may lead to medical breakthroughs. Through examining this amazing adaptability, researchers can learn more about the complex processes that allow the blue-ringed octopus to flourish in its natural habitat and make significant contributions to a variety of scientific fields.

Chapter Three

Distribution and Habitat

Within the genus **Hapalochlaena**, the blue-ringed octopus lives in a range of maritime habitats in the Indo-Pacific area. This section gives a thorough overview of the locations and living arrangements of these unique cephalopods by examining their particular habitats, geographic distribution, and environmental preferences.

1. Area of Interest:

The western Pacific and Indian Ocean coasts are home to the majority of blue-ringed octopus sightings. The following areas are included in their distribution:

- **Australia:** especially in the southern regions of Australia, which include Western Australia, South Australia, and

New South Wales. These regions are frequently home to the Southern Blue-Ringed Octopus (**Hapalochlaena maculosa**).

- **The Philippines and Indonesia:** In these areas, one can find a varied marine environment that is often home to the Greater Blue-Ringed Octopus (**Hapalochlaena lunulata**).

- **Japan:** The Blue-ringed Octopus is found in the waters surrounding Japan, particularly the Ryukyu Islands, where it lives in tidal pools and coral reefs.

- **New Zealand and Papua New Guinea:** These areas are home to blue-ringed octopuses as well, which inhabit environments that are comparable to those in other sections of their range.

2.   Preferred   Environments: Although blue-ringed octopuses can be found in many different marine environments, they are most commonly found in shallow coastal waters, which provide them with plenty of food and hiding spots.

- **Red Corals:** These octopuses are frequently found in coral reef environments, where the intricate structures offer plenty of prey and perfect hiding places. The octopus's life depends on the rich food web that is supported by the colorful and diversified ecosystem of coral reefs.

- **Pools:** Blue-ringed octopuses can be found in tide pools during low tide, where they provide cover and a diversity of small animals. The octopus must adjust to changing water temperatures and levels in tide pools, which present another difficult environment.

- **Muddy and Sand-covered Bottoms:** To evade predators and surprise their prey, these cephalopods also live in muddy and sandy substrates. In these kinds of settings, being able to blend in with the silt is essential for life.

Stone Clefts and Shelled Hideouts: The abandoned shells, rocky crevices, and under rocks are common places for blue-ringed octopuses to take shelter. These hiding places provide defense against hostile surroundings and predators.

3. Environmental Preferences: To maximize their chances of survival and successful reproduction, blue-ringed octopuses have particular preferences for particular environmental circumstances.

Climatic temperature: They favor waters that are warm, tropical, and subtropical, usually between 20 and 30 degrees Celsius (68 and 86 degrees Fahrenheit). The wide variety of marine creatures that make up their food is supported by these temperatures.

- **Depth:** Typically, these octopuses can be found in shallow waters up to 20 meters (66 feet) deep. Shallow waters offer more accessible prey and appropriate hiding spots.

- **Acidity:** Blue-ringed octopuses are marine animals that need salty conditions to survive. Because consistent salinity levels are necessary for their physiological functions, they are usually found in these environments.

4. Adjustments to Diverse Environments:

Numerous adaptations that the blue-ringed octopus has developed allow it to flourish in a variety of dynamic maritime habitats.

- **Stealth:** They can blend in with their environment and evade being seen by predators and prey thanks to their ability to change both color and texture. Their skin contains chromatophores, which enable quick changes in appearance.

- **Spit:** They can efficiently immobilize victims and prevent possible dangers due to their strong venom. The venom is especially helpful in situations requiring prompt and effective predation.

Adaptability and Mobility: Their bodies are soft and flexible, which helps them to fit through tight spaces and intricate reef structures. In a variety of settings, this mobility is essential for hunting and shelter-seeking.

5. Human Impact and Conservation: The habitats of blue-ringed octopuses are significantly impacted by human activity, which presents difficulties for their conservation.

- **Habitat Destruction:** Pollution, destructive fishing methods, and coastal development deteriorate coral reefs and other marine habitats, which reduces the amount of space available for blue-ringed octopuses to live.

- **Changing Climate:** Coral reef ecosystems are in danger of losing their delicate equilibrium due to rising sea temperatures and ocean acidification. The food source and habitat structure of blue-ringed octopuses may be impacted by these changes, which may also cause coral bleaching and biodiversity loss.

- **Pollution:** Plastic trash, oil spills, and chemical pollutants damage marine ecosystems, which affects blue-ringed octopus survival and health. These contaminants have the potential to kill octopuses directly or damage the ecosystems that support them.

6. Environmental Initiatives:

A variety of conservation strategies are required to safeguard blue-ringed octopuses and their habitats.

MPAs (Marine Protected Areas): Important habitats and biodiversity can be preserved via the establishment and enforcement of MPAs. By limiting human activities that harm marine ecosystems, these protected zones enable populations to recover and flourish.

Responsible Behaviours: Reducing the impact on marine environments can be achieved by promoting sustainable fishing and tourism activities. It is crucial to educate the people on the value of conservation and ethical conduct.

Studies and Surveillance: The habitats and populations of blue-ringed octopuses are being studied and monitored continuously, which yields important information for conservation plans. Appreciating their ecological roles and risks facilitates the development of efficient management strategies.

Throughout the Indo-Pacific region, the blue-ringed octopus can be found living in a variety of dynamic and varied marine environments. It is essential to comprehend their adaptations, preferred habitats, and dangers to ensure their conservation. By safeguarding their environments via sustainable methods and conservation initiatives, we can guarantee the existence of these amazing and mysterious animals and maintain their position in the complex network of marine life.

Chapter Four

Reproduction and the Life Cycle

The blue-ringed octopus's life cycle and reproductive habits are intricate and interesting. The life cycle of the blue-ringed octopus is examined in detail in this chapter, along with the complex mating rituals, parental care, and developmental processes that shape its existence from conception to death.

1. Life Expectancy:

The life cycle of blue-ringed octopuses is quite short, usually lasting between one and two years. Their short life cycle is characterized by quick development, early maturity, and a strong emphasis on procreation, which ends with their quick spawning death.

2. Patterns of Mating:

In blue-ringed octopuses, mating is an extremely specialized and occasionally hazardous activity, especially for the males, who frequently run the risk of being misinterpreted by the females as prey.

Relationship: A male blue-ringed octopus approaches a female during courtship, which is the first step in the mating process. Males typically use tactile and visual cues to determine which female is receptive, making them smaller and more wary. To get the female's attention and indicate that he is ready to mate, the male will frequently show off his vivid blue rings.

Misconduct: The male utilizes a specialized arm known as the hectocotylus, which has a groove for delivering spermatophores, or packets of sperm, during copulation. He delivers the spermatophores by inserting the hectocotylus into the female's mantle cavity. The duration of this process ranges from a few minutes to several hours.

Dangers: During this procedure, the male needs to exercise caution because the female could become hostile or ravenous. Males have occasionally been seen running away as soon as they mate to avoid being eaten by the female.

3. Care of Parents and Laying of Eggs:

Following mating, the female blue-ringed octopus begins an important stage of her life: caring for her young and laying eggs. Extreme sacrifice and determination characterize this time.

Laying Eggs: Within an abandoned shell, under a rock, or in a crack, the female deposits her eggs in a protected spot. A female's egg-laying capacity ranges from 50 to 100, depending on the species.

Depressing: The female becomes a dedicated carer after the eggs are laid. She stays with the eggs to protect them from predators and make sure they get enough air. She accomplishes this by using her siphon to gently fan water over the eggs, keeping them aerated and clean.

Offering: For several months, the female does not leave the eggs to hunt or feed during the brooding phase. There is a noticeable physical decrease and weight loss as a result of this self-imposed fast. The female's only concern is ensuring the survival of her young, and she frequently passes away from malnourishment and weariness soon after the eggs hatch.

4. Incubation and Initial Growth:

The life cycle of the species continues with the hatching of blue-ringed octopus eggs, which ushers in a new generation.

Method of Hatching: Planktonic larvae, which are tiny representations of adults, are created after the eggs hatch. Ocean currents carry these larvae, spreading them throughout a large region.

Stage Planktonic: As octopuses transition into the planktonic stage, they are extremely susceptible to predators. They grow quickly and go through various developmental changes as they get older, feeding on minute plankton.

Agreement: In a matter of weeks to months, contingent upon the surrounding circumstances, the larvae descend to the ocean floor. They look for places where they can obtain food and shelter, like rocky crevices, tidal pools, and coral reefs.

5. Growth and Maturation: Considerable growth and behavioral changes occur throughout the transition from planktonic larvae to mature adults.

Infancy Stage: Blue-ringed octopuses start to display the traits and behaviors specific to their species as juveniles. Their characteristic blue rings grow, acting as a warning to would-be predators.

Survival and Extension: Young animals consume a lot of food; they hunt small crustaceans, mollusks, and other invertebrates. Their efficient hunting techniques and high metabolic rate enable them to grow quickly.

Level of maturity: The sexual maturity of blue-ringed octopuses occurs between six and twelve months of age. When they reach adulthood, the cycle starts over, with males looking for females to mate with and females getting ready for the next generation of babies.

6. Ecological Impact and Death:
Despite being short, the blue-ringed octopus's life cycle has a big impact on the environment.

Natural Death and Predation: Predators like fish, birds, and larger marine animals pose a threat to blue-ringed octopuses throughout their lives. Although their strong venom and ability to blend in provide some protection, their natural mortality rate is significant, especially in the early stages of life.

Position inside the Ecosystem: The blue-ringed octopus is an essential component of marine ecosystems, serving as both a predator and a prey. They serve as food for higher trophic levels, and their predation on small invertebrates aids in the regulation of those populations.

Death: The nutrition cycle in their environments is aided by the adult blue-ringed octopuses' death, especially that of the females after they have given birth. As their bodies break down, nutrients are released back into the environment, promoting the growth of other marine life.

The blue-ringed octopus is distinguished by its life cycle and reproductive behavior by its quick growth, strong parental involvement, and amazing ability to balance life and death. Gaining knowledge of these procedures can help us understand the evolutionary tactics that have allowed these amazing animals to flourish in their changing maritime habitats. Scientists can gain a better understanding of the intricacies of marine biology and the intricate interactions between variables that support life in the water by examining their life cycle.

Chapter Five

Intelligence and Behaviour

The blue-ringed octopus is well-known for its amazing behaviour and intelligence in addition to its eye-catching appearance and strong venom. This chapter explores the survival strategies, cognitive capacities, and behavioral patterns that make this little mollusk an intriguing topic for research in animal cognition and marine biology.

1. Patterns of Behaviour:

Activities during the Day and Night: - Activity Cycles: Because they are usually more active at night, blue-ringed octopuses are mostly nocturnal hunters. They typically hide beneath rocks, in cracks, or under shells during the day to relax and evade predators.

Eating Patterns: When they venture out at night to hunt for crustaceans, tiny fish, and other marine invertebrates, their feeding activity peaks. They use a combination of stealth and quickness to capture their victim, approaching it quickly and immobilizing it with venom.

Colour and Texture Changes: - Chromatophores: Blue-ringed octopuses have unique skin cells called chromatophores that give them the ability to quickly change their texture and color. They can blend in with their environment and evade being seen by predators and prey because of this skill.

Aposematic Display: They flash their bright blue rings as a warning when they feel threatened. This is a spectacular aposematic display. By showing their hazardous nature to potential predators, this behavior serves to dissuade them.

2. Mental Capabilities:

Skills for Solving Problems: - Tool Utilisation: Similar to other cephalopods, blue-ringed octopuses have proven to be adept at using tools. They have been seen building shelters or blocking the entrance to their hiding places with shells, rocks, and other things.

Escape Strategies: They are renowned in captivity for their aptitude for breaking out of enclosures, frequently by figuring out how to pry open lids or fit through little gaps. This demonstrates their ability to solve problems and their awareness of their surroundings.

Observational Learning: - Learning and Memory: Octopuses can pick up knowledge by watching other people, according to studies. This capacity for observational learning points to a high degree of social and cognitive learning.

The best ways to hunt and where to hide are among the many things that blue-ringed octopuses can recall with ease. Their capacity to remember and apply prior experiences helps them to survive and hunt more effectively.

3. Interaction and Social Conduct:

Color Displays: - Visual Signals: The primary means of communication for blue-ringed octopuses is visual. To let other octopuses know about their presence, intentions, or emotions, they alter their color and pattern. A warning to rivals or possible threats is given by the quick flashing of the blue rings.

Physical Positions: Apart from alterations in color, body alignments and hand gestures are employed as means of communication. A defensive stance, for instance, may be indicated by an elevated posture and outstretched arms.

Individualism: - Solitary Nature: – Blue-ringed octopuses are primarily solitary animals, only gathering for mating. They rarely engage with other octopuses, but when they do, it's usually to mark territory or show that they're ready to mate.

Reachability: They act in a territorial manner, keeping other octopuses away from their preferred hiding places or hunting grounds. This territoriality lessens rivalry for available resources.

4. Feeding and Hunting Techniques:

Stealth and Surprise: Blue-ringed octopuses are ambush predators, meaning they rely on their ability to stay hidden until they are in a position to attack. They startle their prey by blending into their surroundings thanks to their ability to camouflage.

poisonous Bite: As soon as they are in striking range, they immobilize their prey with a poisonous bite delivered with their pointed beak. The venom is strong enough to paralyze tiny animals almost instantaneously since it contains tetrodotoxin.

Foraging Methods: - Inquiry-Based Behaviour: When foraging, looking through cracks, flipping over rocks, and using their arms to probe for concealed prey, they display exploratory behavior. Their chances of finding food are increased by this methodical and comprehensive approach.

Distinctive Nutrition: Being picky eaters, blue-ringed octopuses frequently favor some kinds of food over others. This selectiveness is probably due to the food value and handling and capture ease.

5. Techniques for Defence:

Hiding and Camouflage: - Avoidance: Their main line of defense is avoidance by concealing and changing their appearance. They can avoid being discovered by predators by using their environment to their advantage.

Uses of Venom: Their deadly bite serves as their secondary defense. Potential predators are cautioned from approaching them due to their toxicity by the vivid blue rings.

Escape Strategies: - Jet Propulsion: Blue-ringed octopuses can quickly flee when they feel threatened by using jet propulsion. They may move quickly through the water by forcing the water out of their siphon.

- Inking: Similar to other octopuses, they can puff up a cloud of ink to form a smokescreen that confuses predators and lets them get away. Additionally, the ink has ingredients that may impair the predator's ability to smell, making it more difficult to locate the octopus.

6. Habits of Reproduction:

Rituals for Mating: - Shows of Courtship: To entice females, guys go on courtship displays. They frequently flash their blue rings and use a variety of arm and body gestures.

Marriage Procedure: Using his hectocotylus, the male transfers spermatophores to the female's mantle cavity during mating. Precise timing and maneuvering are necessary for this process to guarantee successful fertilization.

Involvement of Parents: - Treasure of Eggs: When females protect their eggs until they hatch, it shows a high level of parental investment. They forgo nourishment and their safety to maintain the eggs' cleanliness and oxygenation by fanning water over them.

- Egocentric Conduct: The female frequently dies soon after the eggs hatch due to the extreme concentration on egg care. This selfless conduct guarantees the maximum likelihood of survival for the progeny.

The blue-ringed octopus is an incredibly complex and adaptive species, as evidenced by its behavior and intelligence. These octopuses display a level of cognitive capability that surpasses that of many other animal species, from their sophisticated communication techniques and acute memory to their remarkable problem-solving abilities and strategic use of venom. In addition to advancing our knowledge of cephalopod biology, an understanding of their behavior and intelligence offers important new perspectives on the larger field of animal cognition and behavior research.

Chapter Six

Human-Human Interactions

Humans and blue-ringed octopuses interact in a way that combines curiosity, caution, and occasional danger. This chapter examines a number of these interactions, such as the significance of education and awareness, the dangers and potential medical consequences of an octopus's poisonous bite, and the octopus's place in popular culture.

1. The Interest in Popular Culture:

Iconic Presence: - Visual Appeal: The brilliant blue rings and remarkable appearance of the blue-ringed octopus have earned it widespread recognition and admiration. Its distinct coloring and behaviors have drawn interest from the marine biology community and the general public.

Symbol: Because of its deadly venom and appealing look, the blue-ringed octopus is considered a symbol of both danger and beauty in many cultures.

Books and Media: - **Films and Documentaries:** Many ecological documentaries and films have highlighted the blue-ringed octopus, emphasizing both its intriguing biology and the serious threat it poses.

Readings and Writings: The biology, behavior, and venom of the blue-ringed octopus are covered in a plethora of books and research studies. It's a popular subject for both writers and scholars because of its deadly potential and cryptic nature.

2. Dangers and Health Consequences:

Dangers to Humans: - **Venomous Bites:** Blue-ringed octopuses can be very dangerous to people despite their small size. Their venom contains tetrodotoxin, a strong neurotoxin that, if left untreated, can result in death and paralysis.

Unexpected Meetings: The majority of octopus bites happen when it is handled unintentionally or provoked. The most likely people to come into contact with these octopuses are fishermen, beachgoers, and divers.

Envenomation Symptoms: - Immediate Effects: The first bite is usually painless, but symptoms including numbness, weakness in the muscles, and trouble breathing can appear quickly.

Progression: As the poison spreads, it may result in respiratory failure, generalized paralysis, and maybe even death in the absence of medical attention.

Medication: Antivenom does not exist for tetrodotoxin. Treatment consists of providing respiratory support in particular until the poison is broken down and eliminated by the body. It's imperative to get medical help right away.

3. The Effect of Humans on Conservation:

Dangers to Natural Habitat: - Degradation of the Environment: The habitats of blue-ringed octopuses are seriously threatened by pollution, coastal development, and climate change. Particularly vulnerable are tide pools, coral reefs, and other coastal ecosystems.

Overfishing: Even while fishermen do not usually target blue-ringed octopuses, overfishing other marine species can upset the ecological balance and have an indirect impact on their populations.

Agencies Working for Conservation: - Marine Protected Areas (MPAs): The creation of MPAs can aid in the preservation of blue-ringed octopuses' habitats and shield them from human activity. Fishing, pollution, and coastal development are restricted in certain areas.

Studies and Surveillance: For conservation efforts to be successful, blue-ringed octopus populations must be continuously studied and observed. Effective management tactics can be informed by an understanding of their behavior, habitat requirements, and population dynamics.

Consumer Education: Gaining support for protective measures can be achieved by educating the public about the blue-ringed octopus, its ecological significance, and the value of conservation.

4. Knowledge and Consciousness:

Awareness initiatives: - Public Education: Public education initiatives can educate the public about the blue-ringed octopus, emphasizing the need to be cautious around them and the value of their conservation.

Education Initiatives: Including facts about blue-ringed octopuses in school curricula helps promote responsible behavior in coastal areas and deeper respect for marine life.

Guidelines for Safety: - Safety on the Beach: At beaches and dive locations, educational signage and pamphlets can instruct tourists on how to recognize and steer clear of blue-ringed octopuses. Accidents can be avoided by highlighting how important it is to handle marine life with caution.

First Aid Instruction: It is possible to save lives by offering first aid instruction that covers handling bites from blue-ringed octopuses. It is vital to make sure that divers, lifeguards, and fishermen know what to do in the event of an envenomation.

5. Advantages of Scientific Research:

Medicine Research: - Tetrodotoxin Studies: Studies on tetrodotoxin have important medicinal ramifications. The toxin's capacity to obstruct nerve signals is being investigated for possible uses in the treatment of neurological disorders and pain.

Medicine Development: Novel medications for the treatment of ailments like cardiac arrhythmias, epilepsy, and chronic pain may be derived from components of the venom.

Biological Research: - Participation in Ecosystems: Research on the blue-ringed octopus aids in the understanding of its function in marine environments, including interactions with predators and prey as well as effects on biodiversity.

Adaptations: Researching the special adaptations of the blue-ringed octopus, like its capacity for venom production and concealment, can shed light on animal behavior and evolutionary biology.

Humans and blue-ringed octopuses engage in a variety of relationships, ranging from respect and wonder to caution and preservation.

Promoting healthy coexistence, safeguarding marine ecosystems, and recognizing the singular contributions of this amazing mollusk to marine biodiversity and scientific understanding all depend on our ability to comprehend these relationships. We can minimize the threats to humans who share the coastal domains of the blue-ringed octopus and ensure its continued survival via conservation, research, and education.

Chapter Seven

Marine Ecosystems' Role

The Function in Marine Environments

Despite its diminutive size, the blue-ringed octopus is an important component of marine ecosystems. The ecological significance of the blue-ringed octopus, its relationships with other marine animals, and its effects on biodiversity and ecosystem health are all covered in this chapter.

Dynamics of Predator-Prey:

As Hunters: - Nutrition and Hunting: Carnivorous, blue-ringed octopuses feed on a range of small marine animals, including small fish, invertebrates, and crustaceans like crabs and prawns. These species' population sizes are regulated by their nutrition, which keeps any one group from growing too large and upsetting the natural equilibrium.

Scouting Methods: Blue-ringed octopuses can effectively immobilize and devour animals that can be challenging to capture by using their strong venom. They may take advantage of a variety of food sources due to their capacity to hunt in a variety of habitats, including tide pools and coral reefs.

As Prey: - Risks of Predation: Even though they can be poisonous, larger marine animals including some fish, birds, and other cephalopods feast on blue-ringed octopuses. Though not all of them do, their vivid blue rings act as a warning to potential predators.

Protective Techniques: Their main defense mechanisms include the aposematic display of their blue rings, concealment, and camouflage. These defenses lessen their susceptibility to predators.

2. Interactions with Ecosystems:

Position in Food Webs: - Tropical Level: In marine food webs, blue-ringed octopuses have a mid-level trophic status. They mediate energy transmission between lower and higher trophic levels by acting as both predators and prey.

Cycling for Nutrients: Blue-ringed octopuses aid in the cycling of nutrients in their environments by eating a range of prey and then becoming prey for predators. Following natural death or predation, their remains decay and return nutrients to the environment, sustaining other trophic levels and primary production.

Habitat Sharing: - Symbiotic Relationships: In their shared environments, blue-ringed octopuses frequently participate in both symbiotic and competitive relationships with other marine creatures. For example, they may coexist with animals such as crabs and mollusks and compete with them for food supplies.

Simpler Living Forms: The blue-ringed octopus's skin may be cleaned by some tiny aquatic animals, which eliminates trash and parasites. These interactions demonstrate the interdependence of marine life, despite the lack of thorough documentation.

3. Biodiversity Impact:

Maintaining Biodiversity- Controlling Prey Populations: Blue-ringed octopuses contribute to the preservation of species diversity in their environments by feeding on a variety of marine animals. Because of their predatory tendencies, no single species can become excessively plentiful and outcompete others.

Prime Animal: Blue-ringed octopuses may serve as keystone species in particular areas, essential to preserving the order of their natural groups. The stability and health of the ecosystem may be disproportionately impacted by their actions and presence.

Influence of Habitat: - Changing Microhabitats: The microhabitats in the vicinity of blue-ringed octopuses can be impacted by their activities, which include burrowing and hiding under rocks or in cracks. The distribution and abundance of other marine creatures may be impacted by these changes, which may establish new niches.

Encouraging Complexity in Habitats: Blue-ringed octopuses contribute to habitat complexity, which is essential for sustaining a variety of marine species, by changing their environment. Complex ecosystems increase total biodiversity by providing more resources and cover for a wider range of species.

4. Reaction to Shifts in the Environment:

Flexibility in the Environment: - Adaptability: Because of their exceptional adaptability to many environmental factors, blue-ringed octopuses can live in a variety of coastal and marine settings. They are resistant to some ecological changes because of their capacity to flourish in a variety of settings.

Impact of Climate Change: However, their habitats are seriously threatened by climate change. Their numbers may be negatively impacted by rising sea temperatures, ocean acidity, and habitat loss. Conservation efforts depend heavily on our capacity to comprehend how adaptable they are and how they react to these changes.

Species of Indicator: - Indicators of Environmental Health: Octopuses with blue rings can act as environmental health markers. Their population levels and behavioral changes may be indicators of the wider effects that environmental stresses, such as pollution and climate change, are having on marine ecosystems.

Studies and Surveillance: Data from the observation of blue-ringed octopus populations can be used to evaluate the condition of marine habitats. By putting precautions in place to lessen adverse effects and knowing what influences their populations, conservation methods can be improved.

5. Conservation and Human Interaction:

Human Impact: - Habitat Destruction: Pollution, damaging fishing methods, and coastal development put blue-ringed octopus habitats at risk. To preserve their ecological functions, they must safeguard their surroundings.

Preservation Actions: Protecting blue-ringed octopus numbers and their habitats requires establishing marine protected zones, enforcing fishing regulations, and cutting pollution. Campaigns for public awareness and education can also encourage sustainable relationships with maritime habitats.

Research Importance: - Scientific Understanding: Further studies on blue-ringed

octopuses advance our knowledge of their contributions to and roles in the environment. This information is essential for creating conservation plans that work and guarantee the long-term viability of maritime environments.
Conservation Efforts: Preserving blue-ringed octopuses and their habitats contributes to the overall health of marine biodiversity. By protecting these important species and their habitats, we contribute to the resilience and overall health of marine ecosystems.

In marine ecosystems, the blue-ringed octopus is essential for maintaining biodiversity, predator-prey dynamics, ecological interactions, and environmental health. It is essential for their conservation and the preservation of marine biodiversity to comprehend their ecological significance and the difficulties they confront. By appreciating the significance of these amazing animals, we can endeavor to protect the delicate balance of marine ecosystems and guarantee their continuous existence.

Chapter Eight

Research and Discoveries

The blue-ringed octopus has captivated scientists and researchers for decades, leading to numerous discoveries about its biology, behavior, and interactions with the environment. This chapter explores significant research findings, ongoing studies, and the potential future directions of blue-ringed octopus research.

1. Historical Discoveries:

Early Studies:

- **Initial Identification:** The blue-ringed octopus was first formally described in the early 20th century. Early naturalists were intrigued by its striking appearance and potent venom, leading to initial studies that focused on its taxonomy and physical characteristics.

- **Venom Research:** One of the most significant early discoveries was the identification of tetrodotoxin (TTX) in its venom. Researchers in the mid-20th century isolated TTX and began to understand its potent neurotoxic effects.

Behavioral Observations:

- **Camouflage and Displays:** Early researchers documented the octopus's ability to change color and the purpose of its blue rings as a warning signal. These studies laid the groundwork for understanding its defensive behaviors and communication methods.

2. Modern Research:

Genetic Studies:

- **Genomic Analysis:** Advances in genetic sequencing have allowed scientists to study the blue-ringed octopus at the molecular level. Genomic studies have provided insights into the genes responsible for venom production, camouflage, and other physiological traits.

- **Evolutionary Relationships:** Genetic research has helped clarify the evolutionary relationships between different species of blue-ringed octopuses and other cephalopods. These studies have provided a deeper understanding of their evolutionary history and adaptations.

Neurobiology and Behavior:

- **Cognitive Abilities:** Modern research has highlighted the advanced cognitive abilities of blue-ringed octopuses. Studies on problem-solving, learning, and memory have revealed the sophisticated neural processes underlying their behavior.

- **Sensory Perception:** Research on the sensory systems of blue-ringed octopuses has uncovered how they perceive their environment. Investigations into their vision, chemoreception, and mechanoreception have provided insights into how they interact with their surroundings.

Venom Mechanisms:

- **Biochemical Properties:** Detailed biochemical analyses have elucidated the structure and function of tetrodotoxin and other components of the octopus's venom. Understanding these properties has potential applications in medicine and pharmacology.
- **Venom Delivery:** Studies on the venom delivery system, including the anatomy of the beak and salivary glands, have shed light on how the octopus efficiently immobilizes its prey and defends itself.

3. Ecological and Environmental Studies:

Habitat Use:

- **Habitat Preferences:** Research has explored the preferred habitats of blue-ringed octopuses, such as coral reefs, tide pools, and rocky shores. These studies have highlighted the environmental conditions that support their populations.

- **Impact of Climate Change:** Investigations into the effects of climate change on blue-ringed octopus habitats have revealed potential threats from rising sea temperatures, ocean acidification, and habitat degradation.

Population Dynamics:

- **Distribution and Abundance:** Surveys and population studies have mapped the distribution and abundance of blue-ringed octopuses in different regions. These studies are crucial for conservation efforts and understanding population trends.

- **Behavioral Ecology:** Research on the behavioral ecology of blue-ringed octopuses has examined their foraging strategies, territoriality, and reproductive behaviors in the context of their natural environments.

4. Biomedical Applications:

Tetrodotoxin Research:
- **Medical Potential:** The unique properties of tetrodotoxin have made it a focus of biomedical research. Studies are investigating its potential use in pain management, anesthesia, and the treatment of neurological disorders.
- **Drug Development:** Research into the molecular mechanisms of tetrodotoxin is aiding the development of new drugs. By understanding how TTX blocks sodium

channels, scientists are exploring its applications in treating conditions such as chronic pain and epilepsy.

Biomimicry and Biotechnology:

- **-Camouflage and Materials Science:** The octopus's ability to change color and texture has inspired biomimetic research. Scientists are developing materials and technologies that mimic these capabilities for applications in military camouflage, wearable technology, and dynamic displays.

- **Robotics and Engineering:** The flexible and adaptive movements of blue-ringed octopuses have influenced the design of soft robots. These robots, inspired by cephalopod locomotion, have potential applications in medicine, exploration, and search-and-rescue operations.

5. Conservation Research:

Threat Assessment:
- **Environmental Threats:** Research is ongoing to assess the impact of human activities, such as pollution, overfishing, and habitat destruction, on blue-ringed octopus populations. These studies are essential for developing effective conservation strategies.

- **Conservation Strategies:** Scientists are working on conservation strategies that include habitat protection, sustainable fishing practices, and public education campaigns to mitigate threats and ensure the survival of blue-ringed octopuses.

Public Engagement:

- **Citizen Science:** Public engagement and citizen science initiatives are helping to gather data on blue-ringed octopus sightings and behaviors. These programs involve the public in scientific research and increase awareness of marine conservation issues.

- **Educational Outreach:** Educational programs and outreach efforts aim to inform the public about the ecological importance of blue-ringed octopuses and the need for their conservation. These efforts are crucial for fostering a conservation-minded community.

6. Future Directions: Advanced Imaging: Emerging imaging technologies, such as high-resolution microscopy and non-invasive scanning, are expected to provide new insights into the anatomy and physiology of blue-ringed octopuses.

Genomic Editing: Advances in genomic editing techniques, such as CRISPR-Cas9, may allow researchers to explore the genetic basis of the octopus's unique traits and potentially develop new biomedical applications.

Interdisciplinary Research:

Integrative Approaches: Future research will likely take an integrative approach, combining genetics, neurobiology, ecology, and behavior to provide a comprehensive understanding of the blue-ringed octopus.

Collaboration: Interdisciplinary collaboration among marine biologists, ecologists, chemists, and medical researchers will be essential for addressing complex questions and developing innovative solutions.

Research on the blue-ringed octopus has yielded a wealth of knowledge about its biology, behavior, and interactions with the environment. Ongoing and future studies promise to uncover even more about this fascinating cephalopod, with implications for medicine, technology, and conservation. By continuing to explore and understand the blue-ringed octopus, scientists can contribute to the preservation of marine biodiversity and the advancement of scientific knowledge.

Chapter Nine

Preservation and Guardianship

The blue-ringed octopus is a unique species, and its conservation and protection are essential to its survival as well as the health and richness of marine ecosystems. This chapter lists the main dangers that blue-ringed octopuses face, describes ongoing conservation initiatives, and suggests ways to preserve their habitats and guarantee their existence.

Potential Dangers to the Blue-Ringed Octopus:

Degradation and Loss of Habitat: - Coastal Development: Blue-ringed octopuses are losing their habitat as a result of rapid coastal development. Natural environments like coral reefs and tidal pools are disrupted by construction, land reclamation, and urbanization.

Pollution: Blue-ringed octopuses' habitats are contaminated by marine pollution, which includes oil spills, plastic trash, and chemical discharge. Pollutants have the potential to cause direct harm to these animals or to worsen the conditions in their habitat, making it less livable.

Climate Shift: - Increasing Sea Levels: Sea temperatures rising as a result of global warming may have an impact on blue-ringed octopus distribution and reproductive cycles. Increased heat can also cause coral bleaching, which lowers the amount of habitat that is accessible.

Acidification of the Ocean: Acidification is a result of the oceans absorbing too much CO2 from the atmosphere. This can have a detrimental effect on marine life, especially the blue-ringed octopus species that prey on it. Octopus populations may be impacted in turn by shifts in the availability of prey.

Overfishing and Bycatch: - Direct Catch: Although fisheries do not normally target blue-ringed octopuses, they can be unintentionally taken. Fishing nets and trap bycatch can cause population decreases.

Disturbance of environment: Excessive hunting of other marine animals may upset the natural equilibrium, impacting the accessibility of food and the general well-being of the marine environment.

2. Present-Day Conservation Initiatives:

Marine Protected Areas (MPAs): - Protected Areas: One of the best strategies to protect the habitats of blue-ringed octopuses is to establish MPAs. By limiting certain activities like fishing and coastal development, MPAs protect important habitats and increase biodiversity.

Restricted Areas: Within MPAs, designated no-take zones forbid any form of extraction, offering safe havens where populations of blue-ringed octopuses can flourish unhindered by humans.

Law and Regulation: - Fishing Regulations: Enforcing laws that restrict bycatch and safeguard vital habitats is crucial to the conservation of blue-ringed octopuses. This covers limitations on fishing techniques and equipment that endanger their habitats.

Pollution Control: Measures to curb marine pollution, like restrictions on single-use plastics and stronger regulations on industrial discharge, aid in safeguarding the habitats of blue-ringed octopuses.

Monitoring and Research: - Demographic Research: Data on the location, quantity, and health of blue-ringed octopus populations are obtained through ongoing research and monitoring. Making educated management decisions and evaluating the success of conservation efforts depend on this knowledge.

Evaluation of Habitat: Frequent evaluations of the habitats' health and state aid in identifying regions that require preservation or repair. It's also critical to monitor environmental factors like temperature, acidity, and water quality.

3. Techniques for Upcoming Conservation:

Restoration of Habitat: - Restoration of Coral Reef: Blue-ringed octopuses can gain from efforts to repair damaged coral reefs since there will be more appropriate habitats available. Artificial reefs and coral gardening are two methods that aid in the restoration of these important ecosystems.

Restoration of mangroves and seagrass: Seagrass beds and mangroves are important nurseries for a variety of marine species, and their restoration can improve the general health of coastal ecosystems and help populations of blue-ringed octopuses.

Sustainable Practices: - Fisheries Management: Blue-ringed octopus populations can be safeguarded by supporting sustainable fishing methods such as employing quotas and selective gear that minimizes bycatch.

Eco-Friendly Development: Promoting eco-friendly methods for coastal development reduces the loss of habitat. Reducing the ecological footprint of development projects, utilizing green infrastructure, and preserving buffer zones are some strategies.

Public Awareness and Education: - Outreach Programmes: People can learn about the value of blue-ringed octopuses and the necessity of their protection through public awareness campaigns and educational initiatives. Aquariums, museums, and schools are essential to these initiatives.

Involvement of the Community: Participating in citizen science initiatives and beach clean-ups with the local community promotes protective behaviors and a sense of ownership.

Mitigation of Climate Change: - Carbon Reduction: Reducing carbon emissions is essential for minimizing the effects of climate change on maritime habitats. Policies must focus on improving energy efficiency and making the switch to renewable energy sources.

Modification Techniques: Blue-ringed octopuses are safeguarded against the effects of climate change through the development of adaptation methods, such as the creation of climate-resilient marine protected areas and the restoration of coastal ecosystems.

4. Technology and Science's Role:

Remote Sensing and Drones: Using drones and remote sensing technology for habitat mapping and monitoring yields current and comprehensive data on blue-ringed octopus habitats and environmental conditions. This is an example of innovative research.

Genetic Studies: Studies in population genetics and genomics provide information about the genetic variety and adaptability of populations of blue-ringed octopuses. Planning and management for conservation can be influenced by this information.

Cooperative Efforts:- International Cooperation: Because blue-ringed octopuses are a species that is present in the waters of several different countries, international cooperation is necessary for their conservation. The efficacy of conservation measures can be increased by cooperative efforts.

Transdisciplinary Methodologies: Comprehensive conservation strategies are produced by combining knowledge from the fields of marine biology, ecology, genetics, and environmental science. Complex conservation concerns require interdisciplinary research efforts and collaborations.

5. Achievements and Insights Discovered:

Success Stories in Protected Areas: Case Studies: Examples of effective MPAs where populations of blue-ringed octopuses have recovered emphasize how crucial it is to preserve habitat. Other regions can use these case studies as models.

Community-Led Conservation: Projects that showcase the effectiveness of grassroots activism are those in which nearby communities have assumed a leadership role in conservation efforts. These examples of success demonstrate how important local involvement is to long-term conservation.

Adaptive Management: Experience-Based Learning: The process of conservation is continuous and calls for adaptive management. Conservationists can increase the efficacy of their work by learning from the past and always improving their tactics.

Adaptive Techniques: It is possible to make modifications based on fresh scientific research and evolving environmental circumstances by creating adaptive and responsive conservation methods.

A diverse strategy that takes into account habitat preservation, pollution management, sustainable practices, and public involvement is needed to conserve and protect the blue-ringed octopus. We can guarantee the survival of this extraordinary species and preserve the vitality and diversity of marine habitats by implementing efficient conservation methods, collaborating internationally, and conducting ongoing research. We may encourage group action to save our seas and the species they support by promoting greater awareness and respect for the blue-ringed octopus.

Chapter Ten

Facts About The Greater Blue-Ringed Octopus

- The majority of blue-ringed octopuses are small, with lengths of 4 to 6 centimeters and weights of about 28 grams.

- It is well known for having striking black and blue rings, which intensify in color when the octopus feels threatened or irritated.

- The Southern Blue-ringed Octopus, Hapalochlaena maculosa, the Greater Blue-ringed Octopus, and the Blue-lined Octopus, Hapalochlaena fasciata are the three main species.

- found throughout the Pacific and Indian Oceans, especially in the regions surrounding Australia, Japan, and the Philippines, in tide pools and coral reefs.

- It consumes small fish and small crustaceans like prawns and crabs.

- The tetrodotoxin used by the blue-ringed octopus is strong enough to immediately paralyze and kill its victim.

- There is no known counteragent for tetrodotoxin, which is 1,200 times more lethal than cyanide.

- Blue-ringed octopuses are normally calm and only bite people when provoked, despite their strong venom.

- The main means by which they inject venom into their prey or use it as a defense mechanism is through their beak.

- Scavenging is part of the octopus's diet; to crack open the shells of their prey, they use their powerful beak.

- They only live for two years on average, which is a short lifespan.

- Male blue-ringed octopuses utilize a specialized arm called a hectocotylus to transport sperm to females in their intricate mating behaviors.

- Females only lay eggs once in their lives, and during the time they are caring for the eggs until they hatch, they do not eat and frequently pass away quickly.

- They are renowned for their intellect and have demonstrated sophisticated problem-solving skills by using tools and solving problems.

- They are skilled at camouflage, altering the color and texture of their skin to match their environment and elude predators.

- Marine animals, birds, and larger fish are examples of natural predators.
- The state of blue-ringed octopus conservation is poorly known, yet pollution and habitat destruction are major threats.

- Even though they are little, their venom can cause serious respiratory failure in humans, therefore getting medical help right once after a bite is essential.

- Because of their distinct venom, sophisticated neurological system, and behavior, they are frequently the focus of scientific investigation.

- Campaigns for public awareness and educational initiatives are crucial for promoting conservation efforts and lowering the danger of human contact.

Conclusion

With its captivating look and strong venom, the blue-ringed octopus is an amazing and mysterious animal that never fails to fascinate both the general public and experts. Numerous aspects of this intriguing creature have been covered in this book, including its behavior, biology, and relationships with humans in addition to its vital function in marine ecosystems. We learn about the complicated web of life beneath the waves and the delicate balance that keeps our oceans healthy as we explore the features of this small but powerful mollusk.

It is not only an academic endeavor to comprehend the blue-ringed octopus; understanding it has significant ramifications for marine biology, ecology, medicine, and conservation. The distinct behaviors and adaptations of this cephalopod shed light on neurobiology and evolutionary processes.

Potential biomedical uses of studying its venom include pain management and neurological research advancements. The blue-ringed octopus also acts as an indicator species, showing the effects of human activity and the condition of marine habitats.

Despite its adaptability and perseverance, the blue-ringed octopus has several obstacles to overcome. Its survival and the well-being of the habitats it lives in are threatened by overfishing, pollution, habitat loss, and climate change. To guarantee the long-term survival of marine biodiversity, these risks highlight the urgent need for efficient conservation strategies and sustainable practices.

The blue-ringed octopus has to be protected and conserved by extensive and varied efforts. Crucial actions include creating marine protected zones, enforcing sustainable fishing methods, cutting pollution, and restoring habitats. Furthermore, to promote a culture of conservation and ethical interactions with marine habitats, public awareness and education are crucial. Through community engagement, scientific research, and international cooperation, we can create and implement strategies that effectively protect this remarkable species.

Research and conservation efforts about blue-ringed octopuses appear to have a bright future. Technological innovations like genetic analysis, biomimicry, and remote sensing will expand our knowledge and improve our capacity to safeguard these animals. Multidisciplinary study and cooperation will keep generating creative answers to the intricate problems that marine ecosystems face. Through the adoption of adaptive management and the assimilation of prior achievements and shortcomings, we may enhance our methodologies and more efficiently address new risks.

The fragility and wonder of marine life are represented by the blue-ringed octopus. Its striking blue rings act as a constant reminder of the wonders of nature and the complex web of life that binds us all together. It will need cooperation and a dedication to protecting the natural world for the coming generations to protect this species and its habitat. Everyone has a job to play in protecting our seas, whether it be by backing conservation efforts, taking part in citizen research, or supporting sustainable policies.

To sum up, the blue-ringed octopus is more than just a study topic for scientists; it provides evidence of the variety and adaptability of life on Earth. We fulfill our duty as stewards of the world by carrying out research into, understanding, and protecting this amazing species. To ensure that the vivid blue rings remain to grace our waters for future generations, let the tale of the blue-ringed octopus serve as an inspiration for us to appreciate and preserve the beauty of nature.